..... WHAT'S AT ISSUE? ....

MULTICULTURAL BRITAIN

Paul Wignall

Heinemann
LIBRARY

www.heinemann.co.uk/library
Visit our website to find out more information about **Heinemann Library** books.

To order:
 Phone 44 (0) 1865 888066
Send a fax to 44 (0) 1865 314091
 Visit the Heinemann Bookshop at www.heinemann.co.uk/library to browse our catalogue and order online.

First published in Great Britain by Heinemann Library, Halley Court, Jordan Hill, Oxford OX2 8EJ, a division of Reed Educational and Professional Publishing Ltd. Heinemann is a registered trademark of Reed Educational & Professional Publishing Limited.

OXFORD MELBOURNE AUCKLAND JOHANNESBURG BLANTYRE
GABORONE IBADAN PORTSMOUTH NH (USA) CHICAGO

© Reed Educational and Professional Publishing Ltd 2002
The moral right of the proprietor has been asserted.

Designed by Tinstar Design (www.tinstar.co.uk)
Illustrations by Nicholas Beresford-Davies & Martin Griffin
Originated by Ambassador Litho Lyd
Printed in China

ISBN 0 431 03560 1   (hardback)   ISBN 0 431 03568 7   (paperback)
06 05 04 03 02   06 05
10 9 8 7 6 5 4 3 2   10 9 8 7 6 5 4 3 2

British Library Cataloguing in Publication Data
Wignall, Paul
    Multicultural Britain. – (What's at issue?)
    1. Multiculturalism – Great Britain – Juvenile literature
    2. Pluralism (Social sciences) – Great Britain – Juvenile literature
    I. Title
    306

Acknowledgements
The Publishers would like to thank the following for permission to reproduce photographs:
Bridgeman Art Library: Johnny van Haeften Gallery p9; British Museum: pp28, 32; Commonwealth Institute: p12; Corbis: p18, Bettmann pp4, 19, 24, Adam Woolfitt p10, Richard T Nowitz p16, Danial Laine p20, Lindsay Hebberd p22, Morton Beebe p26, Elio Ciol p29, Christine Kolisch p31 Paul Seheult p36; Cumulus: Gareth Boden p35; PA Photo Library: p27, John Stillwell p11; Panos Pictures: Gar Powell-Evans p40; Rex Features: pp8, 15; Tony Stone Images: Ian Shaw p25; Trip: H Rogers p17, B Turner p30; Tudor Photography: p5

Cover photograph: Bubbles/Frans Rombout.

Our thanks to Julie Turner (Head of Student Services and SENCO, Banbury School, Oxfordshire) and Nandini Mane and Craig Murray from Working Group Against Racism in Children's Resources (WGARCR) for their comments in the preparation of this book.

Any words appearing in the text in bold, **like this**, are explained in the Glossary.

common heritage and a common religion – Christianity. Is that true? Many British people do not have English as their first language, they may speak Punjabi, Urdu or Chinese. People born in Britain may well have parents or grandparents born in Africa, Asia or the Caribbean, Russia, Australia or China. Their religion may be Hindu or Islam; they may be Buddhist or Rastafarian.

A rich mixture

Some people say that anyone who lives in Britain should be taught the 'common heritage' of the English language, English history, English literature and Christianity. But others say that we should be proud of and celebrate our multicultural heritage. We live on an island that is full of different people, all bringing their own background and languages, attitudes and beliefs together into a rich, shared experience.

Britain has always been like this. For thousands of years different people have crossed the sea and settled here. Romans from Italy, Vikings from Scandinavia, Saxons from Northern Europe and Normans from France. More recently people have come from India and Pakistan and from the islands of the Caribbean. There have been **refugees** escaping from wars: Jewish people and Vietnamese, and most recently refugees from the former Yugoslavia. People have come to work or study or get married.

Over time, all of these groups have made their contribution. Place names such as Cirencester or Doncaster remind us that the Romans were here. York, and any town or village ending in -*by*, such as

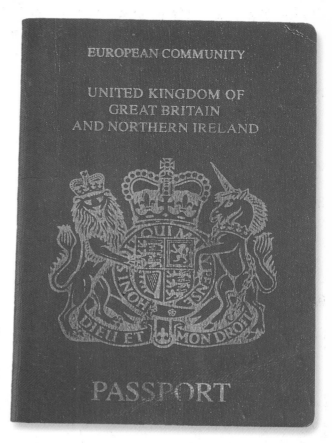

A passport contains information about our public identity.

Whit*by* and Der*by*, are Viking names. Essex and Sussex are places where Saxons settled, while Welsh and Cornish placenames, such as Aberystwyth and Penzance, remind us of those who were in Britain before the Romans arrived. There are Indian, Italian and Chinese restaurants in every town. Even the English language is full of words taken from other languages: Latin and Greek, French, German, Scandinavian, Chinese, to name but a few.

How many different cultures are represented in your school and in your city or town or village?

5

The British Empire

If you look at a map of the world, you will see that Great Britain and Ireland are two small islands at the north-western end of the great land mass of Europe. The earliest European trade was centred on Greece and Italy and merchants came to Britain to buy tin and copper and exchange wine and pottery. About 2000 years ago, when the Roman Empire began to expand, armies, traders and settlers reached Great Britain and what is now England, Wales and southern Scotland became the furthest outpost of Roman rule.

The age of discovery

Empires grow through a combination of military conquest and trade. At first, European trade and conquest was centred on the Mediterranean sea, with Britain on the edge of the known world. But with the European discovery of the so-called

The size of the British empire was drastically reduced during the 20th century.

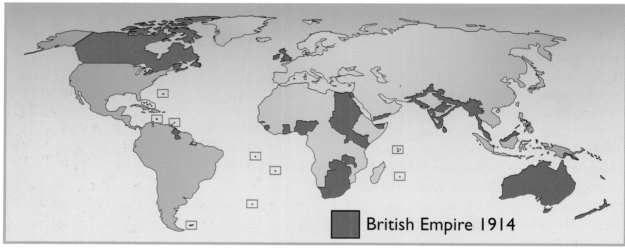

British Empire 1914

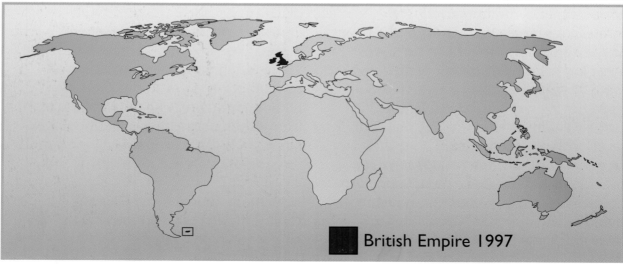

British Empire 1997

New World (the American continent) from the end of the 15th century, it was the countries with best access to the Atlantic Ocean that began to thrive: Spain, Portugal, Holland and Britain.

Gold and tobacco

The first British overseas settlements were commercial enterprises. The Virginia Company was founded in 1606 to search for gold in North America. It was unsuccessful and so turned to growing tobacco, but, just as this venture was about to collapse in 1623, the English government took it over and encouraged the import of slaves from Africa to farm the tobacco crop.

The slave trade

Other companies were established to market other raw materials. By 1670 there were **colonies** in New England, Virginia and Maryland, other settlements in the Bermudas, Antigua, Barbados and Honduras, while the Hudson's Bay Company had begun to trade in north-western Canada. As early as 1600 the East India Company had begun to establish links with India and on through South-East Asia (Penang, Singapore and Malacca). At the same time British interests in the slave trade (to send slaves to the settlements in America and the West Indies) meant that settlements grew in West Africa.

Wealth and power

British merchants traded in a wide range of goods and raw materials: cotton, tobacco, furs, spices, sugar, and later, tea, coffee and rubber were major wealth-earners. The merchants could also **export** finished goods from Britain to the growing colonies of **emigrants** and slaves. The British Navy was strengthened to protect the trade routes and help create further colonies. In 1651 the Navigation Act set up a 'closed economy'. From now on all goods coming into Britain from its settlements and colonies had to be in British ships and all goods going to the colonies had to pass through England. British merchants and the British government soon became among the wealthiest and most powerful in Europe.

BRITAIN AND ROME

Many of the men who were sent abroad from Great Britain to control the countries which became the British Empire had studied Latin and Greek at school and university. This classical education, as it was called, meant that when they were faced with new challenges – such as how to create a legal system or organize schools – they partly looked back to how things had been in Britain, but they also remembered how the Romans and Greeks had done things, and tried to copy them.

Many of the British people living and working in Africa, India or the Far East, for example, actually believed that what they were doing was creating a new Roman Empire – or at least that the British Empire was the successor to that of Rome. When they designed great public buildings, they copied the palaces of Rome or the Parthenon in Athens. They encouraged the study of Latin in schools. When they had their portraits painted, or erected statues in memory of British rulers and officials, they dressed them in togas, looking like a Roman Emperor. And just as the creators of the Roman Empire believed that they were reproducing Rome wherever they went, so the British set about making the countries they were conquering copies of the places they had left behind.

Rule Britannia!

Rule Britannia! Britannia, rule the waves, Britons never will be slaves.

This famous song was written by the Scottish poet James Thomson in 1740. It was written at a time when the British Empire was expanding across the whole world. North America, Africa and Asia all had British **colonies** while Australia and New Zealand were beginning to be opened up by explorers, many of them British. These lines from the song's chorus tell us a great deal. First, they show how the expansion of the Empire was a cause of great national pride: Britain was becoming one of the most powerful nations in the world. Second, the power was a direct result of 'ruling the waves': both trade and conquest depended completely on the strength of Britain's navy, the most powerful in the world. Third, but ironically, while Britons themselves might not be slaves, the Empire was able to grow and prosper only because of the slave trade – a plentiful supply of cheap labour and a ready-made market to buy goods. Finally, Great Britain (the island) was becoming great Britain (powerful and proud Britain), but its political centre was England. The song might have been written by a Scotsman, but it was praising an empire whose centre was London, the capital of England.

The Proms, held in London every year, celebrate British tradition. Artists like James Galway perfom to often nationalistic audiences.

Today the song does not always carry such positive imagery. Some people chant the song as a form of racist abuse implying that white Britons are superior to other races.

Ancient civilizations

As the British Empire expanded, it came into contact with many other cultures. Many of these were very old. Although the British merchants and explorers were often scornful of the people they conquered, thinking of them as little more than animals or undeveloped children, in fact cultures such as those of the native American peoples, African nations, and

the civilizations of India and the Far East were themselves highly developed. And gradually, because trade is a two-way process, not only raw materials such as cotton and tobacco and goods such as clothing and machinery, but also ideas and attitudes passed along the trade routes in and out of British ports.

Tea or coffee?

During the 18th century, Britain became a nation of tea and coffee drinkers. Cheap imports of sugar and cotton changed the habits of British people. The influence of China changed the style of their cups and plates – the word 'china' even came to be used for fine pottery. Imported drugs such as tobacco and opium affected people's health.

At the same time, many people left Britain to live and work in British colonies. Many became very wealthy merchants, while others ran government offices or served in the army and navy or as judges or **missionaries**. While **importing** raw materials, Britain **exported** people and ideas.

Look around you. How much of what we now use every day originally came from parts of the British Empire? What can you add to the list?

An Empire shopping list

Tea, coffee, sugar cane. Bananas, potatoes, cornflakes (corn, or maize, is from America). Sweetcorn, eucalyptus, chocolate. Rubber, teak, mahogany. Gum, tobacco, medicines such as quinine and morphine (which is also a dangerous and harmful drug when used wrongly). Much of what we now take for granted became part of British life as a result of the rise of the British Empire.

Much of the strength of the British Empire was based on trade.

The collapse of the British Empire

The Roman Empire reached its northernmost point at Hadrian's Wall between Newcastle and Carlisle. The Roman province of Britannicum prospered through trade with Europe but Rome, at the heart of the Empire, became even richer. Although Britain declined once the Romans left and the Roman Empire itself collapsed in the 4th century, the foundations were laid for England to grow into a powerful and independent country.

Hadrian's Wall, built between AD121 and 126, was the northern limit of the Roman Empire. Within 200 years, Rome's empire had collapsed.

We can see a similar pattern in the growth and collapse of the British Empire. As trade spread, so did wealth, not only at the centre where London became a huge and imposing city, but also in the various **colonies** and settlements. With the American War of Independence in the 1770s the American colonies separated themselves from British rule. The Empire continued to expand, however, but many of the new countries were increasingly self-governing, even if ruled by people whose roots and allegiance remained British. During the late 19th and early 20th centuries pressure began to grow for greater independence, first for the bigger countries such as Canada and Australia (they had been given limited powers to

manage their own affairs in 1840), South Africa and India, then for the various African and West Indian lands. It was only with difficulty (and partly helped by the invention of the '**concentration camp**') that the British maintained rule in South Africa at the beginning of the 20th century. A massacre of Indian people at Amritsar in 1919 gave added force to calls for the British to leave and prompted the 'non-violent protest' movement of Mohandas Gandhi.

Do as the Romans do…

The Roman Empire had expanded by encouraging the rulers of the conquered peoples to adopt Roman ways and the British Empire did the same. Indian **maharajahs** and African chieftains were sent to England to be educated and the British colonial government formed powerful alliances with them. In India, British rule made little impact on the everyday life of most people, many of whom remained Hindu or Muslim and retained their own language. In countries such as New Zealand, Canada and Australia, where the ruling class was made up of white settlers and their successors, the

earlier culture was much more vulnerable. Although the culture survived, it often did so only as 'local colour' for tourists – the totem poles of native Canadians are comparatively modern inventions, for instance.

A lost empire?

By the middle of the 20th century, the British Empire was crumbling. The countries ruled from London were becoming increasingly independent and, just like the American colonies in the 1770s, saw no reason to have all their decisions made, or at least approved, in London. The **United Kingdom** had been weakened economically by two world wars and was looking towards the mainland of Europe once more for trade. In 1930, Britain still had an empire on which, it was said, the sun never set: it spread all around the world. By 1980, this had almost completely disappeared, although the effects of empire were still felt, both in Great Britain and in the newly independent countries.

The Golden Temple is the holiest shrine of the Sikh religion. On 13 April 1919, British troops fired on a crowd of unarmed Indian protestors here, killing a large number of them. In October 1997, it was visited by Queen Elizabeth II amid tight security: feelings were still running high.

The Commonwealth
of Nations

In 1931 the British government passed a law called the **Statute of Westminster** which gave some of the countries of the British Empire a special status. Many of these were countries such as Canada, Australia and New Zealand whose populations had become dominated by European **emigrants**. The Statute of Westminster created the **British Commonwealth of Nations** and assumed that these specially favoured countries would retain a British style of government and that the British monarch would continue to be their head of state.

The Commonwealth Institute in London promotes awareness of the Commonwealth of Nations through an exhibition of the history and contemporary life of all the countries of the Commonwealth.

Independence

Gradually, countries of the old Empire became independent nations, and many of them chose to retain these less formal links – which were thought to be helpful to maintain trade – when they began to govern themselves. On gaining independence in 1947, India and Pakistan joined the Commonwealth – the first countries with strongly non-European populations to do so. Others decided not to join, such as Burma (Myanmar) in 1948. While others, at the time of independence or later, resigned their membership because of political differences with the **United Kingdom**.

The word 'British' had been dropped from the title in 1946 and the 'Commonwealth of Nations' developed during the 1950s and 1960s as more and more countries became independent.

The Commonwealth of Nations is now a very loose organization with many different forms of government – the British monarch is rarely head of state – but it maintains trading links and cultural connections, which often build on the culture of the British Empire. All major cricket-playing nations, for instance, are or have been part of the Commonwealth, as they were once part of the British Empire.

People sometimes ask what value the Commonwealth of Nations has today. What advantages do you think there might be?

FACTS

The Commonwealth

There are over 50 nations making up the Commonwealth, representing over 1.5 billion people (about one-quarter of the world's population). Some countries are very rich, others among the poorest in the world. At a conference in Harare (Zimbabwe) in 1991, Commonwealth leaders said: 'The special strength of the Commonwealth lies in the combination of the diversity of its members with their shared inheritance in language, culture and the rule of law. The Commonwealth...is uniquely placed to serve as a model...for new forms of friendship and co-operation to all...Its members also share a commitment to certain fundamental principles.

- *we believe that international peace and order, global economic development and the rule of international law are essential to the security and prosperity of mankind;*
- *we believe in the liberty of the individual under the law, in equal rights for all citizens regardless of gender, race, colour, creed or political belief...;*
- *we recognize racial **prejudice** and intolerance as a dangerous sickness...and racial **discrimination** as an unmitigated evil;*
- *we oppose all forms of racial oppression, and we are committed to the principles of human dignity and equality;*
- *we recognize the importance and urgency of economic and social development to satisfy the basic needs and aspirations of the vast majority of the peoples of the world, and seek the progressive removal of the wide disparities in living standards amongst our members.'*

Culture, age and class

Cultures – ways of life and thought, attitudes and beliefs – do not only differ between countries, but there are also differences within countries:

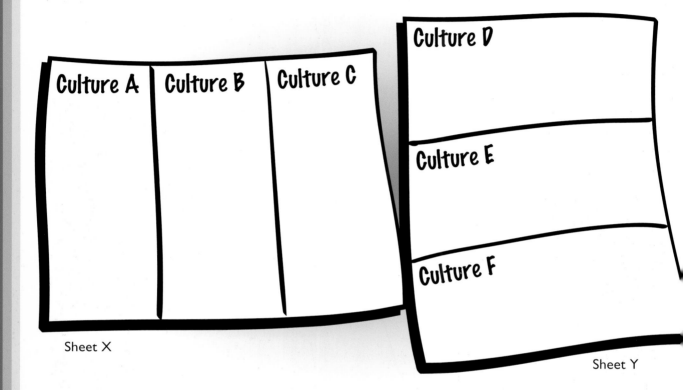

Sheet X

Sheet Y

These differences may be caused by different cultural origins, or be the result of different experiences, age or education, for example. You might like to carry out this experiment. Take two sheets of paper and divide them in three, one horizontally (X) , the other vertically (Y). Now in the right hand column of (X) make a list of things that you are interested in: the sort of music you listen to; your favourite TV programme; a book you like reading; the sport you play or watch; and anything else that you think is part of your **identity**. When you have done that, copy it out into the bottom third of sheet (Y). Now find two people from another cultural background, but the same age as you, and ask them to give their answers to the questions you asked yourself. List their answers in the other two columns of sheet (X). Next, find someone who is about 25 years older than you and someone who is about 50 years older than you. Ask them exactly the same questions and put their answers in the middle and top sections of sheet (Y). Look at the two sheets. Is there more difference between the answers on Sheet (X) or Sheet (Y)? What do you think makes the strongest cultural difference – background or age?

Class and culture

Some people think that 'class' makes an important cultural difference. In other words, that your attitudes will be different depending on whether you are 'upper', 'middle' or 'lower' class. This difference, it is said, can show in the way you speak, what you read and how you think. Class can also be connected with power and wealth. In this way of thinking, education can be very important. Some people think that the school you go to can affect both your class and your culture – you may read different things, have different attitudes to the world around you, and even speak differently depending on the school you go to.

The poet, Tony Harrison known for the political and social elements of his poetry.

The English poet, Tony Harrison, wrote a poem about his own schooldays in Leeds where he felt his teachers sneered at his 'Northern' accent and wanted him to 'talk posh'. English culture, they seemed to be saying, was only for those who lost their own accent. He calls the poem 'Them and [uz]'. '[uz]' here is written in a special script to represent the northern English way of saying 'us'. Do you agree with Tony Harrison?

THEM AND [UZ]

aiai, ay! ay!... stutterer Demosthenes
gob full of pebbles outshouting seas –

4 words only of *mi 'art aches* and...
'Mine's broken,
you barbarian, T.W.!' *He* was nicely
spoken.
'Can't have our glorious heritage done
to death!'

I played the Drunken Porter in *Macbeth*.

'Poetry's the speech of kings. You're one
of those
Shakespeare gives the comic bits to:
prose!
All poetry (even Cockney Keats?) you
see
's been dubbed by [ʌs] into RP,
Received Pronunciation, please believe
[ʌs]
your speech is in the hands of the
Receivers.'
'We say [ʌs] not [uz], T.W.!' That shut
my trap.
I doffed my flat a's (as in 'flat cap')
my mouth all stuffed with glottals, great
lumps to hawk up and spit out ...
E-nun-ci-ate!

(From Tony Harrison, *Selected Poems*,
Penguin Books 2nd edition, 1987, p 122)

The Jewish community in Britain

There have been Jewish people in Britain for over 1000 years. The first Jewish people to arrive probably came as Roman soldiers and officials – and maybe even as slaves. There may have been Jewish communities in Bedfordshire, Exeter and York. After the end of the Roman Empire we hear no more for certain about Jewish people in Britain until 1075 when we know that some were living in Oxford. There are also Jewish people mentioned in the **Domesday Book** (1086) in Oxfordshire and Dorset.

An **orthodox** Jew teaches Hebrew to a child in Jerusalem. Learning the Law (or Torah) has always been the centre of Jewish religious belief.

FACT

The Jewish people have always been a people whom other nations have found hard to accept. Their commitment to their religion, with its strong moral sense based on God's law, the Torah, has made them stubborn in many of their attitudes to life. Their moral strength has often been an unwelcome challenge to others. Their separateness from other societies has led to suspicion and persecution. Despite all this, they have survived to worship God in the **synagogue***, to keep the Sabbath (Saturday) as a holy day, and to live as a strong community, as committed to one another as to their God.*

Persecution

Jewish people in Britain at this time, as everywhere in Christian Europe, and for centuries to come, were outcasts, persecuted and frequently unprotected by law. Even though the first followers of Jesus had been Jewish people, the Christian Church came to believe that Jewish people were not God's chosen people, but God's enemies. As the church became more powerful, so attacks on Jewish people increased. But because of a ban on Christians lending money for profit ('usury'), Jewish people were allowed to take up this way of life.

With some local difficulties, Jewish people were able, in fact, to live generally peacefully in Britain until 1189 when a massacre followed a trivial incident at Richard I's coronation. A number of other attacks followed, in Norwich and York. Although King Richard tried to give Jewish families some legal protection, their situation became worse until, 100 years later, on 18 July 1290, a **decree** was issued expelling all Jewish people from England.

Jewish people began to return to England, some posing as Portuguese Christians, around 1500, but were expelled again in 1609. By 1630, however, there was a secret synagogue in Creechurch Lane in London. Increased tolerance of Jewish people was one of the results of Oliver Cromwell's parliament and in 1655 there was a public celebration of Rosh Hashanah (the Jewish New Year) in London. Jewish people

The interior of a synagogue – the Jewish place of worship.

continued to be persecuted and ill-treated, however, and their very difference from the communities around them was a source of suspicion.

A great asset

In the 19th and 20th centuries many Jewish people fled to Britain from persecution in Europe, and especially from **Nazi**-occupied Europe. Even in Britain they have had to cope with intolerance and **prejudice**, in particular from Nazi sympathizers both before and after the Second World War. Despite their persecution over the centuries, Jewish people have made a great contribution to British life. Benjamin Disraeli was a 19th-century Conservative Prime Minister while Emmanuel Shinwell was a Labour MP for 40 years in the 20th century. Many Jewish people have worked in the medical and legal professions. Others have worked in the arts, including the sculptor, Jacob Epstein, and one of the founders of British ballet, Dame Marie Rambert.

Multicultural Britain before the 20th century

Black people almost certainly first arrived in Britain from North Africa with the Roman armies 2000 years ago. Some may have married and stayed in the country, though no black community was established. Other individuals, also of African descent, would have come as

traders or with ambassadors from other European countries. In those times there was little obvious **prejudice** against black people. They were seen as exotic and unusual, but rarely a threat, although William Shakespeare, in his play about a black general, *Othello*, does have Othello's enemies describe him in language we would still regard as racist.

By 1780 London was a thoroughly multicultural city. There were communities of Jewish, Irish and French **immigrants** as well as many people of

This 1840 painting by J M W Turner shows the terrible practice of slave ships throwing their human cargo overboard at times of danger. But Turner is saying something else as well: it was painted at the very end of the slave trade – it is slavery itself that is being dumped overboard.

African descent. Most Africans were the servants of merchants from the **colonies** or of captains of slave ships. It was fashionable to have a black servant. Some had probably been born in Britain – Britain had traded in slaves for nearly 200 years. In September 1731, the City of London ordered that no black person could become an **apprentice**, after an incident where a black apprentice carpenter called John Satia had been granted the '**freedom of the city**' and so gained the right to vote.

By 1780 there were also a few slaves who had been released in America and then escaped to Britain. There were even a few actual slaves in Britain – slavery was not illegal at the time and cities such as Bristol and Liverpool still held slave auctions.

Driven to protest

In early June 1780 there were riots in Britain. These were at first specifically against Roman Catholics, but then there was a general riot against the government in protest against poor and repressive living conditions. Over 300 people were arrested and at least three were described as 'black' – Charlotte Gardiner, John Glover and Benjamin Bowfey. Charlotte was later hanged when no one came to speak on her behalf. John Glover and Benjamin Bowfey, although found guilty, were not hanged because their white masters came and asked for mercy. These incidents tell us that there was already a small population of black people in London, as well as other cities and towns in Britain, long before the 20th century, and that they have been ill-treated and discriminated against for a very long time.

MUSICAL INSPIRATION

Samuel Coleridge-Taylor was born in London in 1875. His father was from Sierra Leone in West Africa, his mother was English. Coleridge-Taylor's father qualified as a doctor but racial prejudice kept patients away and he returned to work in Africa. Samuel became a well-known musician and composer. Many of his compositions explored African music and ideas and his work greatly influenced many American musicians and gave them the confidence to make their own music.

Samuel Coleridge-Taylor's father was an African doctor. Samuel was a composer influenced by African music whose work was popular in the early 20th century.

Invited immigration in the 20th century

This is a Rastafarian band. Rastafarians are proud of their black heritage. The movement began in Jamaica and it is named after Ras Tafari who was crowned the Ethiopian Emperor Haile Sebrassie I. One of the things Rastafarians do to remind them of their homeland, is let their hair grow naturally into dreadlocks. This represents the lion of Judah, which is also a symbol for the Emperor.

The British Empire depended upon the slave trade for its prosperity and, even when slavery was abolished in British **colonies** early in the 19th century, there remained a clear division between the rich white landowners and the poor black workers. The British also organized the movement of this cheap labour from place to place, not only in the form of

black people from Africa to the West Indies, but also Asians from India to South and East Africa and the islands of the Caribbean, and from the islands of the South Pacific to Australia.

As more and more countries gained their independence, this manipulation of the labour force became more difficult, and British control of the market to buy and sell goods around the Empire also came to an end. At the same time, after the Second World War there was a severe shortage of workers for unskilled jobs in the **United Kingdom**, especially in hospitals and transport. British governments encouraged one final transfer of cheap labour by offering the chance of work to people from the West Indies, India and Pakistan in particular.

A hostile reception

In June 1948 an old troop ship, the *Empire Windrush*, arrived in London with 510 people from the West Indies on board. At first they were prevented from landing by the government, but eventually they were housed in a large air-raid shelter on Clapham Common before moving into houses in Brixton. These became the core of the African-Caribbean community in Britain. White British people were anxious for their jobs, and disturbed by the prospect of mass immigration, a government minister, Arthur Creech Jones, tried to calm the panic by saying that the newcomers 'won't last one winter in England'.

A tense situation

In the 1950s and 1960s immigration from the West Indies, and later from India and Pakistan, was encouraged by the British government, which was looking for cheap sources of labour for unpopular jobs such as nursing and transport. The numbers of **immigrants** grew: 60,000 arrived in 1960 and 120,000 in 1961. Communities were established in many towns and cities – especially Brixton and Southall in London, St Paul's in Bristol, Manningham in Bradford, and in Leeds. Racial tension increased. There were race riots in Nottingham and Notting Hill Gate in London.

Why does it exist?

The tension between the different communities is partly economic: the fear of white workers that 'they' will take 'our' jobs. Although the British Empire was largely a thing of the past, white people retained a false sense of superiority over the new **ethnic** communities.

Many of these new communities retained and developed a strong sense of their own culture, made even stronger by isolation and the need to survive economically and practically. There are, too, considerable differences between communities with their origins in Africa and the West Indies on the one hand, and those whose **ancestors** came from Asia on the other. These differences are made harder to overcome by the system of Empire whereby Asians were used to oversee the work of people of African or Caribbean origin in plantations, farms and factories. In this way as in many others the negative effects of the British Empire are still felt today.

India and Pakistan

The British Empire was built on trade and slavery. Although the slave trade was abolished and slaves **emancipated** early in the 19th century, the demands of trade still required cheap labour. In the islands of the West Indies, for example, this could be provided by the former slaves and their **descendants**, but in other parts of the Empire, especially India, different solutions had to be found. From about 1835 until 1916, many poorer Indian people (both Hindu and Muslim) were **'indentured'** to landowners across the Empire. This happened in Mauritius,

This celebration of Divali is in India but many British towns and cities keep the festival in November, with processions and decorations.

Guyana, Trinidad and Jamaica for work on sugar plantations; in Ceylon (Sri Lanka), Malaya (Malaysia) and Burma (Myanmar) for tea, coffee, and rubber plantations; in East Africa to help build railways; and in South Africa for mining and cotton. Although badly housed, overworked and underpaid, the Indian communities stuck together and recreated their social and cultural life in their new environments.

The Sikhs

Although poor labourers and farm workers were among the earliest groups to leave India, they were quickly followed by others. Many members of the Sikh community from the Punjab region, a community with a strong military history, first joined the police and the British army and were sent to other parts of the Empire. Some travelled to Australia, but were denied entry under anti-immigration laws passed in 1901 so moved on to Canada where many worked in the timber industry.

Partition

In 1948 the British left India and the country was divided into two separate nations: India and Pakistan. Pakistan was itself divided into two and East Pakistan eventually became the country of Bangladesh. In 1949 there were fewer than 8000 Indian and Pakistani settlers in Britain. In the next few years the numbers grew very slowly, mainly from the displaced Sikh population (the **partition** of India ran through the Punjab). In 1955 only 7350 people came to Britain from India and Pakistan.

Throughout the 1950s it was difficult for Indian or Pakistani people to come to Britain. The Indian and Pakistani governments often refused passports, making travel impossible. Also, migration was for economic reasons and to join family members. The **United Kingdom** was attractive only for the economic opportunities it gave. Just as previous generations had recreated their social and cultural lives in their new settings, so did those who began to settle in Britain.

Numbers grew after 1960 when the Indian and Pakistani governments began to issue passports again. At the same time, Britain was booming, with jobs and opportunities much more easily available. In 1961, 48,850 people arrived in Britain from India and Pakistan.

Racism

The first generation of people arriving in Britain from India and Pakistan experienced the same racist attacks and **discrimination** as those who had travelled from the West Indies. All the black and Asian communities were vulnerable, often living in areas of poor housing, with schools and other services unable to meet their cultural or religious needs, and put under pressure to do low-paid jobs in bad working conditions. By the 1980s most members of the black and Asian communities had been born and educated in Britain, and expected to work, marry, have children, grow old and die in Britain. The 1980s also saw the development of anti-racist and equal opportunities policies in all areas of British life. But **racism** and discrimination has not gone away. Who is a Briton? White and Christian, wearing a skirt or a suit? But a Briton may also be Hindu or Muslim, wear a turban or a kanga or a sari!

Multicultural communities

In reality all the major towns and cities of Britain are multicultural. They are made up of many different communities with a wide variety of attitudes, beliefs, religious practices, diets, sporting and artistic interests, attitudes to education, and languages. Some communities mix with others, some are deliberately separate. In this, British cities today are like every other city around the world, and most cities throughout history.

Life in the city

Cities are multicultural communities. They depend upon trade. Through employment opportunities they encourage people to move in and look for work, or set up shop on their own. If you look at a map of the city of London today you will see that, despite all the rebuilding after the destruction of the Second World War, its shape is still essentially that of the London which Shakespeare knew and through which Queen Elizabeth I travelled. That city was divided into small sections where groups of people engaged in similar activities lived. There were areas for carpenters, for fish merchants, for butchers, for weavers

Cities are multicultural communities. New York in 1900 was made up of people of many different origins: Chinese, Jewish, African, and from most European countries.

or for printers of books. Some of these specialist trades were often conducted by people from other countries. There were communities of the French, the Dutch and the Portuguese. Later Chinese and Jewish communities emerged. Later still, and certainly by the end of the 20th century, there were communities from Jamaica or Barbados, Ceylon, Pakistan and Bangladesh.

Each of these communities makes its own contribution, not only to the commercial life of the city by what it makes, buys and sells, but also by its attitudes and beliefs. In a major city such as London or Edinburgh, Bristol, Liverpool or Cardiff there are followers of every imaginable religion (even some newly invented ones), speakers of almost every major language, skilled performers of music, dancers, writers and thinkers from every part of the world. As they live together, so their enthusiasms and explorations rub off on one another.

A 'living website'

People sometimes say that the Internet has made the world smaller. But in a great city the rest of the world is often just around the corner. In a country like Britain, which is itself very small, the multicultural life of London has spread to most other towns too. Look around you. How many cultures – religions, languages, ways of eating, ways of celebrating, music and dance, sports and ideas – can you find? Look carefully. You will be surprised just how many there are. Towns and cities are living websites of ideas and attitudes just waiting for you to explore them.

Modern life is a living website of differences to explore and celebrate.

25

The impact of the United States

The second half of the 20th century has seen the idea of a world empire move from the **United Kingdom** to the United States of America. For some of that time, the USA was in competition with the Soviet Union for influence, but with the collapse of the power of Russia in the late 1980s, the field has been left open for the United States, the powerful successor of those small **colonies** that broke away from British rule at the end of the 18th century.

The Americanization of culture is truly a world-wide phenomenon, but one which has a particular impact in Britain. More than half of television programmes, and far more than half of all films shown in British cinemas were made in America. The clothes we wear are dominated by American fashion: baseball caps, jeans, trainers. The food we eat – deep-pan pizzas and burgers – was largely invented in American cities. Many of the largest international companies are based in the United States: Coca-Cola, Nike, Microsoft, Disney, McDonald's, Levi Strauss, to name but a few.

All the same

The selling points for American products are their inexpensiveness, their quality and their consistency. In the early 1900s Henry Ford created the production line approach to car manufacture – where each worker did one job, time after time, rather than a team of workers making a complete car. Ever since, the American industrial process has been guided by what are called 'economies of scale'. This means that the more you make of something, the cheaper it can be, and the easier it is to make identical copies of it. This model of

American films and television are key elements in contemporary culture.

industry has been copied throughout the world and is now true not just for cars or computer software, it is also true for burgers and even the bags of fries that go with them – standard sizes, 'regular' or 'large', and a standard taste. No matter where you are in the world, a McDonald's burger will taste the same because the 'Mcworkers' doing the 'Mcjobs' will have been trained in exactly the same way to use exactly the same ingredients!

More different than we think

British culture is particularly open to Americanization (or vulnerable to it, depending upon your point of view), not only because of our imagined historical ties with the United States but also because of our sense of a shared language. In fact neither of these is particularly true.

America has come a long way since the **Declaration of Independence** in 1772. Many other cultures have contributed to its development. Disney films retold German and Central European stories, for example. Even pizzas and burgers, American inventions though they are, are based upon Italian and German originals. And although we do share a common language – English – it is also true that Spanish-speakers are close to being in the majority in many parts of the United States.

The big issue

Nevertheless, American culture has undoubtedly become the dominant force in the world in the past 20 years. This has been reinforced by the growth of personal computing software and the Internet. It is worth bearing in mind

Bill Gates, the man behind the Microsoft empire.

though, that in many parts of the world not only are there few personal computers, there is no electricity with which to run any computers. Some people think that American culture, committed as it is to measuring success by wealth, is in danger of making us forget that for many people having enough to eat is a bigger issue than whether to choose 'large' or 'regular' fries.

We can also ask what impact American film and television has had on race relations in the **United Kingdom**. In some films we see different races co-operating with one another – and this may help to reinforce co-operation and respect in our country too. But other films show violence and racial hatred – either as fiction or, in documentaries and news programmes, as fact. Do you think these programmes encourage racial violence and hatred? Or do they shock us into doing what we can to make sure such scenes of hatred never happen here? What do you think?

27

The European Union

One of the ongoing arguments between British politicians in the early 21st century is whether we should be 'in' or 'out' of Europe. In many ways this is a strange argument. We only need to look at a map to see that the British Isles are a set of small islands off the north-west coast of Europe. Britain's position on the coast of the Atlantic gave it many advantages in creating an empire through trade by sea, advantages which it took for over 300 years. Today, however, world power has shifted to the United States. Isn't it sensible, some people say, for Britain to return once more to establishing good trading and political relationships with its European neighbours?

Our European neighbours

On the other hand, there are those who argue that Britain's influence in the world can best be maintained by close ties with the United States with whom it shares some common history (though not a great deal) and a common language (though Spanish is now nearly as important a language in the United States as is English). Perhaps, too, the long history of distrust and war between the **United Kingdom** (and especially England), France and Germany has made British politicians suspicious of too close a relationship with our European neighbours. But it is worth remembering here that King William I was French, King William III was Dutch and King George I was a German who spoke very little English and our present royal family is directly descended from this German king.

A traditional view of the relationship between England and France? 'The British Lion and the French Cock', a sketch by Philippe de Lontherbourg, c 1797.

Economic realities have, since the Second World War, forced the United Kingdom to work closely with its European neighbours, who had themselves created close economic ties from 1952 and formed the **European Economic Community (EEC)** in 1958. The United Kingdom stayed outside the EEC until 1973.

How close should we get?

In 1991 the Treaty of Maastricht committed all the member states of the newly created European Union (EU) not only to economic co-operation but also to closer political ties, a stronger European parliament and system of justice and, eventually, a shared currency, the Euro. As a member of the EU, the United Kingdom must make sure that its laws, its social and economic and defence policies, for instance, fit in with the policies of its European partners and follow agreed standards. For instance, European regulations say how many hours someone can work before they have a break, or how many days they can work before they must be given a day off.

There are many who disagree with this closer union with other European countries. Some English politicians even argue that we should leave the European Union altogether, believing it is still possible for Britain to stand alone in the world, or at least have closer ties with the United States. In a speech to the Conservative Party conference in 1995, Lord Tebbitt quoted a song by Michael Flanders and Donald Swann to give us his view of Englishness:

> 'And crossing the channel one cannot say much
> For the French or the Spanish, the Danish or Dutch;
> The Germans are Germans, The Russians are red
> And the Greeks and Italians eat garlic in bed.
> The English are moral, the English are good
> And clever and moral and misunderstood...'

Do you agree? Or do you think, like those who disagreed with Lord Tebbitt, that this sort of **prejudice** is not helpful in the modern world because it is unjust and discriminatory?

The European parliament building, Strasbourg.

Globalization

The growth of the British Empire both stimulated but also depended upon an attitude to people as consumers. The British Empire was one big market place in which people bought and sold. From the very beginning, however, with the Navigation Act of 1651 that required all goods to be shipped through Great Britain or on British ships, it was British merchants who stood to make most money out of the arrangement.

Free trade?

The phrase often used for this sort of arrangement is '**free trade**' or, in more recent times, 'the power of the market'. This assumes that people want to buy and sell, that they will do so for the best price, and that they should be free to do so. The argument sounds a good one. After all, if you have something and I want it, can't we bargain for a price – and the more I want it, the more I'm going to be prepared to spend. But what if I 'persuade' you to sell it for less than it cost you by holding a knife to your throat? Or what if you 'persuade' me to spend all my money on it by twisting my arm up my back? Is that free trade?

Many of the products we now buy are of a standard quality and are produced at a low cost by global companies.

Unfortunately, the British Empire's view of free trade was rather like holding a knife to someone's throat. The power of the British navy meant that British merchants could make traders in India or Africa 'an offer they couldn't refuse'. The British Empire was hardly unusual in this – it is the way empires tend to work: trade and conquest go hand in hand.

The power of the TNCs

Today we are in a similar situation, but the pressure to buy and sell is put on us – and by 'us' we can now mean 'the whole world' – by big **transnational corporations (TNCs)**, which are increasingly taking power away from individual nations. A theory of **economics** alternative to free trade argues that countries should be encouraged to create their own internal manufacturing and **import** and **export** as little as possible. But TNCs – whether they are selling burgers, jeans, computer software or television soaps – want to place their products in as many countries as possible. TNCs create standard products in huge quantities and this **mass-production**, often done cheaply in poor countries for low wages, floods the market and drives out more expensive but locally produced goods.

Needs versus wants

Another claim for free trade is that it increases competition: if more than one person is trying to sell you something, you can choose the best deal. TNCs, however, may have the power to buy out the competition and sell their goods at whatever price they think people are prepared to pay. When this is linked to aggressive advertising campaigns which make people want their products, it can

Many TNCs use people and children in poor countries to produce goods and pay only a very low wage.

reinforce poverty or create wants which may have very little connection with needs. How many people who want a mobile phone actually need it? Or can afford it? Or buy one, and then are unable to afford the line rental or the call charges?

How many of the things that advertisements try to persuade you to buy do you actually need, or even want? And how many of the things in your house or classroom were actually made in your own country?

What is a nation?

John Dixon's 1774 mezzotint shows Old Father Time revealing a glorious future to Britannia (here representing England), Hibernia (Ireland), Scotia (Scotland) and America. But within five years the Empire would begin to collapse with the American War of Independence.

The Romans called it Britannicum, but until 1604 this island (the eighth largest in the world) off the coast of Europe was made up of several nations – England, Scotland, Wales, Ireland and Cornwall – which gradually came to be controlled by the English crown. When James VI of Scotland followed Queen Elizabeth I as

King James I of England, he was proclaimed 'King of Britain' – a new title, but one thought to date back to the time before the Romans came. By the 1740s, after the formal Act of Union which made England and Scotland a single nation, it was common to speak of the peoples of these islands as 'British' and the empire they were creating around the world as the 'British Empire'.

Identity

What is a nation? First, it is a way of creating a sense of **identity**. People who share a common language and attitudes, and perhaps a common history, who have the same laws and religion – these may be a nation. But often this sense of identity is something invented by politicians. They may choose to refer back to an imaginary past – as King James did when he decided to be called 'King of Britain'. He imagined he was recreating a unity lost to those who lived in Great Britain (the island) when the Romans invaded.

Freedom

Second, a nation may be something invented to provide focus in a fight for freedom from oppression or tyranny. As people begin to see themselves as different and special, so they want to be seen by others as different and special. Out of everything that has happened to them, they create a history – a story of their own past – and they begin to value their own language, their own customs and attitudes. Cultures conquered by powerful neighbours fight back and claim independence. Many modern nations – Switzerland, Poland and Norway, for example – were created in just this way, as were many countries that gained independence from the old British Empire.

Exclusion

Third, the idea of a nation may be an invention to try to exclude other people. In this sense, politicians and others argue that one group of people alone have the right to call themselves British, or French, or whatever. All others – **immigrants** or incomers – are then excluded and even thrown out. This much more negative view of a nation was a major factor in **Nazi** Germany's attacks on Jewish people, gypsies and homosexuals. Tests may be created to decide who is in and who is out. The Nazis looked at people's birth certificates to see if they had Jewish ancestors. More recently in Britain a Conservative politician, Lord Tebbitt, said that one test of being British was to ask which international cricket team you supported. Unless it was England, you should not be seen as British.

But some people say that, even if it was once possible to speak about being 'British', it is not any more. The 'British' Empire, they say, was really the 'English' Empire, ruled from London, and the **United Kingdom** of England, Wales, Scotland, Northern Ireland (and, some would add, Cornwall) is itself crumbling away. In 1994, 75 per cent of people who lived in Scotland said they would describe themselves as 'Scottish' and not 'British'.

Do you think we should describe the people who live on these islands as 'British'? How would you describe them? How do you describe yourself?

Devolution

Britain today is, as it has been for hundreds of years, a society made up of people from many backgrounds, languages and cultures. England is only one of the kingdoms which go to make up the **United Kingdom**. The others are Wales, Scotland, Ireland, and some would add a fifth, the ancient kingdom of Cornwall. Even within these countries there are regions with their own separate sense of identity: the Highlands and Islands of Scotland are very different from the Lowlands, near the English border; in North Wales, Welsh is more commonly and naturally spoken than in South Wales; in England, there is often a sense of great pride in being from Newcastle, or Birmingham, East Anglia or Somerset.

A UNITED KINGDOM TIMELINE

1536 England and Wales joined as a single nation

1604 King James VI of Scotland also becomes King James I of England

1707 The Act of Union makes England (and Wales) and Scotland a single nation

1801 Ireland joins the United Kingdom

1922 Southern Ireland (Eire) gains independence

1997 Referenda in Wales and Scotland come out in favour of devolution

1999 Scottish and Welsh assemblies begin with limited powers to make their own decisions

What is devolution?

Devolution is the transfer of political power from the centre to the regions. The United Kingdom has a single Parliament at Westminster, in London, in England. Although Members of Parliament come from right across the United Kingdom, and over the years there have been Welsh and Scottish Prime Ministers as well as English, still some people have felt that the decisions that were taken were often of greatest advantage to the English, at the expense of the regions. Sometimes they have felt, too, that the further away from Westminster an area was – such as the islands of the Hebrides or the far west of Cornwall – their needs were less likely to be heard.

The United Kingdom Parliament is dominated by political parties – especially the Labour and Conservative parties – who expect their MPs to vote for what the party wants, rather than according to the local wishes and needs of the people who elected them. Parliament may claim to be putting the 'national' interest first but many Scottish, Welsh and Irish politicians claimed this actually meant putting the English interest first. In the light of this, the British government was put under pressure to ask the people of Wales and Scotland directly if they would like **local assemblies** that would be able to make limited decisions for the well-being of local people. The first referenda were held in 1979. Not many people in Wales and Scotland actually voted – only about one in three – and of these the vast majority of Welsh people said they did not want any local assembly, while just over half of those who voted in Scotland said they did. This was not felt to be a strong enough vote to go ahead.

Scottish and Welsh assemblies

The arguments did not go away, however. Scottish and Welsh voters tended to return Labour MPs but while the Conservative government was in power for the 1980s and most of the 1990s this meant that many Scottish and Welsh people felt they were not being listened to or helped. When the new Labour government came to power in 1997, it immediately arranged for new referenda. This time Scottish voters were strongly in favour, but Welsh voters voted 'Yes' to a Welsh assembly by only a very narrow margin. The new assemblies began their work in 1998 with limited powers for local decision-making, although most major decisions are still taken at Westminster.

The Labour government is discussing the possibility of 'regional assemblies', say in the North of England, or the South-West, to make decisions in England along the lines of the Scottish and Welsh assemblies. Do you think this is a good idea? If you live in Wales or Scotland, do you think the assemblies in your country have made any difference?

British people embrace a range of backgrounds and cultures.

Ireland

Ireland is the smaller of the two main islands that make up the British Isles. The history of its links with its larger neighbour, Great Britain, is complicated and painful. Ireland was a separate kingdom until the 12th century when the Pope gave the English King, Henry II, the right to be its lord. After England became a Protestant country in the 16th century, attempts were made to impose this form of Christianity on the strongly Catholic population of Ireland. Much blood was shed and bitterness created.

Many Protestant families were moved from England to live in Ireland and community divisions were created that are very deep and hard to heal.

A wall in Belfast painted with Republican slogans showing IRA members in 1919 and 1982.

A divided Ireland

After an Act of Union in 1801 made Ireland part of the **United Kingdom**, Irish people argued, without success, for the right to manage their own affairs. An uprising beginning in 1916 led to a partition of Ireland in 1920 and the creation of the 'Irish Free State' in the south of the island in 1922. This was later called the Republic of Ireland or Eire.

Northern Ireland, sometimes referred to as Ulster, has continued to be a part of the United Kingdom. There have been times when Northern Ireland has been given the power to manage its own affairs, but the deep divisions between some members of the Roman Catholic and Protestant communities have meant that co-operation has often been difficult, and at times impossible. They have led to a great deal of misery and killing.

Working towards peace

In 1985 the Anglo-Irish agreement gave the Republic of Ireland a share in political and legal matters in Northern Ireland. Since 1997 the British and Irish governments have succeeded in getting the political leaders of the two communities to find some common ground and work towards sharing power. But the deep suspicion – and often open hatred – between some members of the Protestant and Roman Catholic communities is still a powerful force.

Common interests

In Northern Ireland, within the United Kingdom itself, we can see what happens when cultures collide and are unable to find common ground because of **prejudices** that have grown over many centuries. And yet, despite these divisions, there is much that unites not only the communities of Northern Ireland, but also the Northern Irish with those Irish people south of the border. Ireland may be officially divided, but support for Irish rugby and other sports crosses all the divisions, as does love of traditional Irish music.

But the search for those things which unite Ireland goes deeper. The efforts to find a political solution to end the violence and distrust have been matched by attempts to encourage young people to understand one another, and live together peacefully. One important product of this work for peace is the Corrymeela community, a group of Protestants and Catholics based at Ballycastle in Northern Ireland who are committed, in their own words, to "provide opportunities for meeting, dialogue and learning… to dispel ignorance, prejudice and fear and to promote mutual respect, trust and co-operation". The Corrymeela community works in schools and communities, and is also active in protecting and supporting the victims of violence or those living in fear.

The Irish contribution

Ireland, too, has contributed much to the cultural life of the United Kingdom. The Irish poet, Seamus Heaney, is read in schools throughout the United Kingdom and the writer Roddy Doyle's novel *Paddy Clarke, Ha, Ha, Ha*, published in 1993, is a wonderful story of a boy growing up in Dublin.

(At least) four countries

The wonderful diversity of cultures that goes to make up the **United Kingdom** can be seen wherever we look.

England

The flag of England is St George's cross – a red cross on a white background. England's footballers and rugby players usually wear white, either with a badge of three lions or a red rose. The red rose is a very old symbol of Englishness. In the Wars of the Roses during the 15th century, the red rose was the symbol of the House of Lancaster while the white rose represented the House of York. Sporting fixtures between Lancashire and Yorkshire are still often called 'Roses matches'.

England's patron saint is St George and his special day is 23 April, also celebrated as the birthday of England's greatest poet and playwright, William Shakespeare. English people may well sing 'Rule, Britannia' when cheering their side on, or at times of national celebration. The words were written in 1740 at the height of the British Empire.

Wales

It is probably only a coincidence that England's patron saint, St George, killed a dragon and that the dragon has been, since the beginning of the 19th century, a symbol of Wales. Red is Wales' colour – the red dragon and the red shirt worn by famous rugby players such as Neil Jenkins and footballers such as Ryan Giggs. Other Welsh symbols are the daffodil and the leek – a flower and a vegetable. The Welsh patron saint is St David and his special day is 1 March. Welsh people are famous for their singing and 'Land of our Fathers' is one of their favourite songs.

Scotland

Scotland's colour is blue and the best-known symbol is the thistle – a prickly plant that represents a willingness to defend oneself against enemies. The national flag is a white diagonal cross – called St Andrew's Cross after the patron saint – on a blue background. It, too, is part of the Union Flag. Scottish national songs include 'Flower of Scotland' and 'Scotland the Brave'. True Scotsmen wear the kilt on special occasions, including 'Burns Night', a celebration of the Scottish poet, Robert Burns, which takes place every year on 25 January.

Ireland

Ireland's patron saint is St Patrick, whose day is celebrated on 17 March. It is celebrated especially in the United States where so many families of Irish origin live. Ireland's colour is green and on St Patrick's day, some rivers and streams are filled with green colouring. The national symbol is the shamrock, a three-petalled leaf.

Many of these symbols and songs are only used when groups of people gather together for sporting events or other celebrations. In recent years, and under the influence of the film *Braveheart*, a romantic and fanciful account of the Scot William Wallace, people have also taken on such occasions to painting their face with the national colours. Perhaps this has some link with the ancient custom of inhabitants of the British Isles of painting their faces blue with a dye called woad before going in to battle. Some old customs return in very surprising ways!

The future of nationalism

We live in a complex world where many cultures compete for our attention. Television documentaries, films and the Internet all allow us to enter different worlds. We may let them pass us by without paying too much attention, or they may have a strong impact on us, or they may even change our attitudes and beliefs.

The world, too, is in many ways a smaller place. International media, and the huge **transnational corporations (TNCs)** such as Coca-Cola and Microsoft, influence almost everyone's lives. It is quite possible

Shopping is now an international business. But who decides the prices? This is a supermarket in Ulaan Bataar, Mongolia.

40

that people in Bournemouth and Bogota, Manchester and Manila will be wearing the same style of baseball cap or trainers, or be eating an almost identical burger or bag of regular fries while watching the same soap opera on TV.

Breaking up

Towards the end of the 20th century large groups of **nation states**, such as the British Empire and the Soviet Union, broke down into their smaller components. Countries such as Yugoslavia divided along cultural lines: Bosnia, Croatia, Slovenia and so on. Even the **United Kingdom of Great Britain and Northern Ireland** (to give it its full title) is increasingly functioning as a group of separate entities – England, Wales, Scotland and Northern Ireland.

The end of the world as we know it?

In the light of this, some people say the very idea of the nation is doomed. They think the world of the future will be many separate countries. They may share a language or a religion or a common history (or they may only be linked by geography) and will be dominated by the TNCs, backed up by the armed forces and power of the United States of America. To put it another way, some people believe that, just as the Roman Empire needed its army and the British Empire needed its navy to maintain enough peace for trade to flourish, so in the future TNCs will look to the United States to create an environment for global trade.

Or a new beginning?

But other people take a very different view. They think that, although in the short term the smaller countries may be very vulnerable – and often very poor –

there is a possibility that over a longer period of time, new and more just societies can develop. These people argue that, just as earlier Empires, such as those of Rome and Britain, created wealth from which in the end everyone benefitted, so the Empire of the TNCs will raise standards of health and education throughout the developing world. What do you think?

A third way

TNCs depend on an ever-expanding market in which to sell their products. They need growth. But there is another way, and this is the way of **sufficiency** – a world where enough is enough and where small is beautiful. The alternative to **globalization** may be to make small countries increasingly self-sufficient, and from this base, to enjoy the good things we can give to one another.

Traditionally a nation has been defined by what separated it from other nations: people of the same cultural origin, speaking the same language and practising the same religion. But modern nations have to recognize that they will contain people of different cultural backgrounds, different languages and religions. The question then is: how does a nation learn to celebrate and make use of these differences while making sure that people can live together happily, with justice and equal opportunities for everybody. Perhaps the most successful nations of tomorrow will be the ones that are most truly multicultural.

Just a dream? What do you think the world will be like in fifty years time? Will there be a lot of small nations, or just a few large ones, or will the idea of the "nation" have disappeared altogether – will the future be in the hands of the TNCs?

41

Celebrating difference

In a book full of fun, but full, too, of insight, the American writer, Bill Bryson, looks at Britain in the 1990s. Everywhere you go, he says, in *Notes from a Small Island*, everything looks, sounds, and even tastes the same. In every town, shopping precincts (what Americans call 'malls') are full of the same chain stores, selling the same goods to people who are often dressed in very similar ways. Inside the shops there may be background music that will hardly differ from place to place. After shopping we may go to one of several fast food outlets or coffee shops, then go home to watch television programmes made by a small number of companies on very similar themes and in almost identical styles.

Cultural tourism

Some people call this 'supermarket culture'. As we walk down the aisles of a supermarket, it may look as though there is a huge choice, but look more closely. Two things have happened. First, there is not a great deal of real choice. All the supermarkets will probably have the same things on their shelves, even if the packets look slightly different. And second, although the goods may promise original tastes and authentic flavours, in fact they have often been carefully changed, processed and made more bland.

Cultures are different – often very different – from one another. There is a great danger, though, that trying to enjoy other cultures, even those very close to our own, becomes another version of supermarket shopping, or what is sometimes called cultural tourism. That is to say, the apparently 'foreign' or even 'exotic' experiences have been subtly changed, toned down, made less shocking or disturbing, less different.

There is a danger, too, that even a multicultural experience will become just another way in which the **transnational corporations (TNCs)** such as Nike or McDonald's sell their products to us. Again, are they really offering more choice, or just the same thing in a different packet?

Up to us

But there is still a world we can explore and learn from. Underneath the global campaigns of the TNCs the new, smaller countries, proud of their cultural roots and independence, are struggling to survive. The 21st century can give us a world dominated by TNCs in which in the name of choice the rich will get richer and the poor get poorer, while all cultures collapse into one Disneyworld. Or we can make a world that loves and celebrates differences, where people can go out exploring and really find new cultures and new experiences, learning and growing by being part of the rich diversity that life has to offer. The choice is ours.

This symbol of Fair Trade – a greater equality between the countries of the rich North and poor South – could stand for all hopes for multicultural exchange and celebration: One World but Many Experiences.

Glossary

ambassador the official representative of one country in another

ancestors earlier generations of your family or nation – for example, your grandparents and great grandparents, or the people who lived in your country in the past

apprentice a young person being taught a special skill or trade

assembly a group of people meeting together to make decisions

British Commonwealth of Nations an organization of over 50 nations joined together for friendship and trade whose main link is that they were all once part of the British Empire

colony a group of people who have settled in a foreign country

concentration camp a prison camp set up for people (often of the same ethnic group) whom the government of a country wish to keep separate or to kill

Declaration of Independence the document drawn up in 1776 by the first states of the United States to proclaim their separation from the United Kingdom

decree an order or a law given by someone in authority

descendants people who will come after us – for example our children or grandchildren

discrimination to treat someone differently, and less favourably, because of their ethnic origin, their gender or their religion, for example

Domesday Book a book drawn up for William the Conqueror to show who owned what land in England, and its value

economics the study of money and finance

emancipate to set someone free – used, for example, to refer to laws which set slaves free

emigrant someone who leaves their home country to go and live permanently in another country

European Community (EC) the member states of the European Economic Community: Belgium, Denmark, France, Germany, Greece, Holland, Irish Republic, Italy, Luxembourg, Portugal, Spain, United Kingdom

European Economic Community a "common market" – a special grouping of countries with a special trading relationship formed in 1957. The first countries in the EEC were Belgium, France, Holland, Italy, Luxembourg and West Germany. They were joined in 1973 by Denmark, the Irish Republic and the United Kingdom, in 1981 by Greece, and in 1986 by Spain and Portugal.

European Union (EU) the new description from 1993 of the member states of the European Union. Austria, Finland and Sweden joined in 1995. The EU has its own parliament in Strasbourg, makes its own laws – which all the member states must accept – has its own court (the European Court of Justice) and its own currency (the Euro).

export sending goods abroad to be sold

"freedom of the city" a special honour given to people by a town or city in recognition of their service to that place

free trade an agreement allowing countries to trade with one another without having to pay high taxes when importing them

globalization something which puts international concerns above those of individual nations; often used to describe the way in which large companies or other organizations can dominate small countries

identity knowing who you are and where you come from

immigrant someone who has come to live permanently in a country

import bringing goods into a country in order to sell them

indenture the legally binding agreement between a master and an apprentice

maharajah an Indian prince or ruler

mass-production making goods in great quantities using standard processes (for example, the assembly lines used to make cars)

missionary someone with a religious belief who travels to another culture to try to persuade other people of its truth

nation state a political unit based upon a single language, culture or religion, or upon a shared territory

Nazi a member of the National Socialist party which, under Adolf Hitler, ruled Germany between 1933 and 1945

orthodox somebody who sticks to accepted views of something, especially in religion

partition dividing up; it can mean a dividing up of a country into separate parts – for example the creation of India and Pakistan in 1947

prejudice thinking badly of someone without good reason; making assumptions

racism treating someone badly because of their colour or ethnic origin

referendum (pl, referenda) asking everyone entitled to vote in a country to answer an important question. For example, in 1973 a majority of the people of the United Kingdom voted "yes" when asked if they wished to join the European Economic Community. In 2000 the people of Denmark voted "no" when asked if they wanted to replace their currency (the krone) with the euro.

Statute of Westminster the law agreed by the United Kingdom Parliament in 1931 which allowed some countries of the British Empire (for example Canada) to have their own governments

sufficiency having enough

synagogue the place where Jewish people meet to worship God

transnational corporation (TNC) a big business or company which operates in many different countries, for example Coca-Cola, Mcdonalds, Ford and Sony

United Kingdom of Great Britain and Northern Ireland (UK) the political union of the four once-separate kingdoms of the British Isles

Contacts and helplines

CHILDLINE
Freepost 1111
London
N1 0BR
0800 1111

THE CITIZENSHIP FOUNDATION
Ferroners House
Shaftesbury Place
Aldersgate St
London EC2Y 8AA
020 7367 0500
www.citfou.org.uk

THE COMMISSION FOR RACIAL EQUALITY (CRE)
Elliot House
10-12 Allington Street
London
SW1E 5EH
London *020 7828 7022*
Edinburgh *0131 226 5186*
Cardiff *029 2038 8977*
www.cre.gov.uk

THE CORRYMEELA COMMUNITY
8 Upper Crescent
Belfast
Northern Ireland
www.corrymeela.org.uk

RUNNYMEDE TRUST
133 Aldersgate Street
London
EC1 4JA
www.fhit.org/runnymede/

THE UNITED NATIONS
www.un.org

Other campaigning organizations:

THE EUROPEAN MOVEMENT
200 Buckingham Palace Road
London
SW1W 9TJ
www.euromove.org.uk
The European Movement is dedicated to the future of co-operation between European countries.

THE INSTITUTE FOR CITIZENSHIP
62 Marylebone High Street
London
W1M 3AF
www.citizen.org.uk
The Institute is committed to helping young people understand the importance of active citizenship, which may range from being a good neighbour to running a major campaign.

Further reading

Non-Fiction

Britain and the Slave Trade
Rosemary Rees
Heinemann Ed, 1995

Living Through History:
The Making of the United Kingdom
Britain 1750-1900
Twentieth Century World
Nigel Kelly, Rosemary Rees, Jane Shuter
Heinemann Library 1998

The Making of the United Kingdom
J Scott
Heinemann Educational, 1992

Modern Britain
A Langley et al
Heinemann Library, 1994

Troubled World: The Troubles in Northern Ireland
Ivan Minnis
Heinemann Library 2001

Turning Points: The End of Apartheid
Richard Tames
Heinemann Library 2000

What's at issue: Citizenship and You
Katrina Dunbar
Heinemann Library 2000

What's at issue: Prejudice and Difference
Paul Wignall
Heinemann Library 2000

World Beliefs and Cultures:
Buddhism
Christianity
Hinduism
Islam
Judaism
Sikhism
Sue Penney
Heinemann Library, 2000

Fiction

Divine Wind
G Disher
Signature 1999

The Fire Children
E Maddern
Frances Lincoln 1994

Girl in Red
G Hicyilmaz
Orion 2000

Grania O'Malley
M Morpurgo
Mammoth 1996

Hope Leaves Jamaica
K E Ernest
Mammoth 1994

The Other Side of Truth
B Naidoo
Puffin 2000

The Real Plato Jones
N Bawden
Puffin 1995

Smash!
R Swindells
Puffin 1998

Tough Shadows
J Lingard
Puffin 1999

Index